A World OF Difference

12 men and women whose
faith helped change their world

Bob Hartman
Illustrated by Anna-Marie Glover

© Speaking Volumes 2017

Published 2017 by CWR, Waverley Abbey House, Waverley Lane, Farnham, Surrey GU9 8EP, UK. CWR is a Registered Charity – Number 294387 and a Limited Company registered in England – Registration Number 1990308.

The right of Bob Hartman to be identified as the author of this work has been asserted by him in accordance with the Copyright, Designs and Patents Act 1988.

For a list of National Distributors, visit www.cwr.org.uk/distributors

Editing, design and production by CWR.

Illustrations by Anna-Marie Glover.

Printed in the UK by Linney.

ISBN: 978-1-78259-764-3

Contents

Mother Teresa

For some people, life can be very hard. So hard, it's tricky to imagine. But you can do it, if you try.

Imagine, for a start, that you have nowhere to live. No roof above your head. Where would you go if it rained, or turned cold?

Now imagine that you have no way to make any money. How would you buy the things you really need, like food to eat?

Now imagine that you were ill, perhaps very ill. You have to pay to see a doctor and to receive medicine where you live, but because you have no money, you simply can't afford them. How would you get better? How would you cope with any pain you might be feeling?

Finally, imagine you were so ill that you were dying. Imagine that you were all alone, with no family or friends to comfort you...

The sad truth is that there are millions of people, all around the world, whose lives are just like that. There was a woman who dedicated her life to helping them. Let's pretend for a moment that we can go back in time and visit her at work and hear her tell her story...

Shhh… We need to be nice and quiet. I'll have to keep my voice down. I'm caring for a few poorly people here today. It's so good of you to visit. Who am I? My real name is Agnes, but people know me as Mother Teresa. You may think that's strange, especially given that I don't have any children – but perhaps once you've heard my story, you might understand why people call me 'Mother'.

Let's start at the beginning, shall we? I was born in 1910. My family is Albanian but we lived in what is now the capital city of Macedonia. My parents were devout Catholics, and I grew up hearing stories about Catholic missionaries. They were people who travelled all around the world, helping others and telling them about Jesus. I decided that I wanted to be a missionary, too. As a Catholic, the best way to do this was to become a nun – to dedicate my life to Jesus, and promise never to marry, so that all my energy and time could be given to serving Him.

When I was 18, I left home and moved to Rathfarnham in Ireland. And, sadly, I never saw my family again.

Sorry. Let me just give this person their medicine. There we go.

Catholic nuns are also called 'sisters'. We live together in groups, which are called 'orders'. I joined the Sisters of Loreto, who lived in Loreto Abbey. There, I trained to be a nun, and learned English. Then, when I was 19, I went to help at the school my order looked after in Calcutta. All the way from Ireland to India!

I taught in the school, learned the local language, Bengali, and continued my training. In 1931, when I was 21, I took my vows, which means I made my promises to God and officially became a nun. As a part of that, I had to choose a new name. That's right! Can you imagine? What would you change your name to?

Most nuns choose the name of a particular saint they admire. In the Catholic Church, saints are people who have been good examples of what it means to follow Jesus, and who have also seen miracles. It usually takes a long time for the Church to make someone a saint. You have to have done some pretty remarkable things.

As I had always wanted to be a missionary, I decided to take the name of Saint Thérèse of Lisieux, who is the patron saint of missionaries. The problem was that another nun at the school had already chosen that name. To avoid confusing everyone, I used the Spanish version of Thérèse, which is Teresa. So, known as Sister Teresa, I taught at the mission school for 20 years.

But every time I walked the streets of Calcutta, I couldn't help but notice the poor, helpless people who lived there. People without homes, or food, or medicine, or anything, really.

The more I saw of them, the sorrier I felt for them. Then, one day, I realised that God was asking me to help those people. I believed He wanted me to form a new community of nuns, dedicated to making a difference in their lives. I know that Jesus helped those who were ill and ignored by others, so surely He would want me to help the poor and the suffering, too.

And that is when I left the Sisters of Loreto and became Mother Teresa. I received basic medical training and, along with 13 other nuns, went to live among the poorest of the poor in Calcutta. It was also then that I exchanged the nun's habit I had worn at the school for simple Indian clothing – the white sari with a blue trim that I'm wearing today.

It was really hard, at first. I had to plead for

food and for everything else that I needed to care for people. There were even times when I wondered if I should have just stayed at the school. It would have been much, much easier. But I was confident that God wanted me to do this, so I carried on. And in 1950, I was given permission by the Church to form my own order, The Missionaries of Charity, dedicated to helping people who feel unwanted, unloved and uncared for throughout society. With that as my goal, I established this hospice here in Calcutta. In this place, anyone can receive care when they are dying.

I've also started a special hospice for people with leprosy. It's a type of disease that causes nasty sores and eventually stops you from feeling whatever touches your skin. It's infectious, which means you can easily catch it off someone else. That's why people with leprosy are often avoided. Not here, though. We take them in and care for them, just as we would for anyone else.

As more and more nuns have joined me, and as more and more donations have been given, we have been able to do more and more for the people we serve. We work hard to protect and defend human life, such as the lives of unborn or abandoned children, and so we've built orphanages and shelters for homeless children. We care for those who have had to leave their country because of war or a natural disaster. We look after blind people, and those with other disabilities. And, we're doing this not only in India, but in many other places across the world.

So let me tell you, listening to God and following Him was the best thing I could have ever done. I played a part in His plan to help His children who are in need. I don't have any of my own children, that's true. But, through my work, I've been able to be like a mother to thousands.

I'd better get back to them now, actually. There's lots to do!

Mother Teresa's world-changing story didn't stop there. Her little group of 13 nuns eventually grew to over 4,000, helping people in around 120 different countries!

When bad things happened, like earthquakes and wars and disasters, she was there to lend a hand. And she and her blue and white sari were instantly recognised, all around the world.

She met many famous people, including the Queen of England, but she never let that distract her from her God-given purpose to live among the poorest of the poor, and care for their needs. She even received the Nobel Peace Prize in 1979, and gave the prize money, of course, to the poor.

After she died in 1997, the process was set in motion by the Catholic Church to recognise her as a saint. (It takes a long time, remember?) In 2016, 19 years after her death, it happened. Pope Francis led the ceremony, and the Albanian girl who had taken the name of a saint, became a saint herself. Saint Teresa of Calcutta.

George Cadbury

So then, what's your favourite Cadbury chocolate? A Flake? Wispa? Creme Egg?

People didn't always have the choice of chocolates we have today. And, awful as it may seem, there was a time they didn't have chocolates at all! Someone had to create them. And one of those people was a man called George Cadbury. Let's look at snapshots of his life, faith and, yes, chocolate...

George's story actually begins with his father, John, who started selling drinking chocolate in the early 1800s. You would go into John's shop in Birmingham, which also sold tea and coffee, and he would grind up cocoa beans for you. The beans had to come all the way from Africa and the West Indies, so only rich people could afford to buy cocoa. Still, there was a good market for it, so John experimented with ways to make it better. He created blocks of cocoa that people could buy and take home with them. It wasn't like powdered drinking chocolate today. You had to scrape a bit from the block of cocoa into your cup, and then add hot milk or water.

John Cadbury was also quite good at making people aware of the things he had for sale. So his cocoa became very popular. He moved into a small factory, and then into a bigger one, and by 1842 he was producing 16 different kinds of drinking chocolate.

This made John happy for two reasons. His business was successful, for a start. But the other reason was to do with his belief in God. He was a Christian who belonged to the Society of Friends, or Quakers. Quakers really wanted to help people who were poor. In John's day, it was quite common for some men to spend a lot of their wages in pubs, so much so that there wouldn't be enough left to care for their families. John believed that by providing an alternative to alcoholic drinks, he was helping those families. This was especially important when the British government made cocoa more affordable for everyone.

Things seemed to be going well for the Cadbury family, but then, in the 1850s, the business began to struggle. John fell ill, and in 1861, he had to retire. John's sons, Richard and George, took over. They were only 25 and 21. For the first five years, running the business was very difficult indeed. In fact, they nearly gave up.

But in 1866, they found a way to make their chocolate better! And that made all the difference.

The cocoa butter in the drinking chocolate they had been making gave it a very strong taste, so it had to be mixed with other ingredients, like the starch from potatoes – or some chocolate makers even added brick dust! You wouldn't want potatoes or bricks in your chocolate, would you? And neither did they. In fact, George Cadbury himself described their drinking chocolate as a 'comforting gruel'. Not very appealing, is it?

The fact was that they simply needed to make a better product. So, in 1866, the Cadbury brothers visited a chocolate maker in Holland who had a machine that could squeeze the cocoa butter out of the cocoa beans. It was perfect! With less cocoa butter in their cocoa, they no longer had to mix it with potato starch. It was purer. It tasted better. And it could be made into fine powder, much like cocoa is today. Better still, they found a way to take that cocoa butter they had squeezed out of the beans and turn it into what we know as milk chocolate. They shaped it into bars. They made all sorts of fancy filled chocolates. They packed them into decorated boxes. And people *loved* them!

The business grew bigger than it had ever grown before. So big, in fact, that they needed a new factory. And that's where their Christian faith made a big difference to the plans they made. Like their father, George and Richard were Quakers. They could have built their new factory somewhere in the middle of Birmingham, but they knew living conditions there were not good.

The houses were small and overcrowded, which also made it easy for disease to spread.

Richard and George knew that Jesus cared for the poor and wanted them to care for people, too. So, in 1878, they bought land four miles south of Birmingham, in what was then the country, and built the new factory there. But not just a factory. They built a village! Combining the name of the nearby river Bourne and the French word for 'town', they called it Bournville (which today is the home of Cadbury World!). In contrast to the cramped city houses, these homes were light and airy, with beautiful gardens. And the rents were not expensive. Working people could afford to live there. George and Richard built places for the people in the village to eat, as well. And they constructed sporting grounds. They were determined that their employees should live happy and healthy lives.

When Richard sadly died in 1899, George continued to run the increasingly successful chocolate business – and come up with even more ways to improve life for his employees. He created committees so his workers could make comments about the company, and suggest changes. He started a bank so they could save their money and earn interest on it. And he made it possible for them to take courses and further their education.

George's work to make things better for people wasn't confined to his business. The wealthier he grew, the more influence he had. He used some of his money to buy the *Daily News*, a national newspaper that had been founded by Charles Dickens. And in that newspaper, he opposed the things he disagreed with politically, like certain wars. He also campaigned to bring an end to sweatshops, where people worked long hours, in terrible conditions, for hardly any money at all. And he argued for something that didn't exist in his time – pensions. He wanted to make sure that everyone had money to live on when their working days were over.

What does any of this have to do with chocolate? It has everything to do with it. For George Cadbury took the profits he made from selling confectionary and used them to make life sweeter for everyone. He may have died in 1922, but his legacy lives on. The next time you see

a Cadbury advert – or better yet, take a bite of some of their chocolate – why not remember George and his family and think... what could you do to make a difference to the world around you?

Harriet Tubman

Just for a minute, pretend that you own a cat.

And if you do own a cat, then you don't have to pretend!

Now pretend that your cat just had kittens. You own the kittens, right? They belong to you, because the cat belongs to you. So you can keep one of the kittens, if you like. And you can sell the rest, or give them away. It's up to you.

Now imagine that what you own is not a cat, but a person. That person belongs to you. Their children belong to you, too. And if you want to sell one or two of those children to someone else, you can. Even to someone who lives far, far away. Because, like that cat, they are your property.

It's hard to imagine or believe, isn't it? It's shocking! But for millions of African slaves, living in America in the early 1800s, that is exactly what life was like. They were property, who were bought and sold, and whose families were split apart, as easily as you would sell one of your cat's kittens to someone on the other side of town.

Harriet Tubman was one of those slaves. She lived an extraordinary life...

Harriet was born in the 1820s. Her mother, who was also called Harriet – or 'Rit' for short – was owned by a white woman called Mary Brodess. Harriet's father, Ben Ross, was owned by a white man called Anthony Thompson. Mary and Anthony married, and they brought their slaves into their new home, along with their furniture and dishes and pots and pans, and everything else they owned.

Eventually, Rit and Ben married, too. And, sometime later, their daughter Harriet came along.

Except, she wasn't called 'Harriet'. Not at first. Her full name was Araminta Harriet Ross, and everyone called her 'Minty'.

Minty's life as a slave girl was very hard indeed.

Three of her sisters were sold, by her master, to a family that lived far away.

She was put in charge of watching a tiny baby, and every time the baby cried, Minty was beaten. The scars she received from those beatings stayed with her for the rest of her life.

When she grew older, Minty worked outside, driving the oxen who pulled the ploughs, and checking muskrat traps (muskrats are four times as big as normal rats!).

And she didn't always do this at home. In those days, a slave owner could lend his slaves to a nearby farm, like he'd lend a rake or a wheelbarrow or anything else that belonged to him. That's what happened to Minty sometimes, and she wouldn't see her family for ages.

But the worst thing that happened was when Minty went into town to fetch supplies. She ran into another slave, who had left the fields without asking permission. His master was chasing him, and called out to Minty to stop the slave. Minty didn't do that, so the slave owner threw a two-pound weight that hit Minty in the head. The blow didn't kill Minty, but for the rest of her life she suffered terrible epileptic fits.

Minty did not go to school, but her mother told her stories from the Bible. She was particularly fond of the stories about Moses, who led the people of Israel out of slavery and into the freedom of the promised land. This not only inspired Minty's faith in God, but also the hope that she too might one day be set free.

When Minty was in her twenties, she married a man called John Tubman, and that is when she began to call herself Harriet. In Maryland, where

Harriet lived, not every black person was a slave – and her husband was one of the free men. But even though he was free, Harriet still legally belonged to her master. And when her master died, things took a turn for the worse. There was a very real chance that everyone in her family would be sold off, one by one, to different people in different places. So Harriet decided that this was the time to escape!

On her first attempt, she went with two of her brothers, who decided, in the end, to return. But when she tried again, she went without them, and she successfully reached Pennsylvania, a state just across the northern border of Maryland, where people were not allowed to own slaves.

How did she do it? She used what was called 'The Underground Railroad'.

The Underground Railroad was not a real railroad, with tracks and trains. It was a series of houses, dotted all around the slave-owning states, where runaway slaves could hide. By night, brave volunteers would lead the runaway slaves from one house to the next, taking them ever closer to the states where they could live free. The houses were like stations on a real railroad, and the volunteers were called 'conductors'.

This is what Harriet had to say about the moment she passed over the border into freedom: 'When I found I had crossed that line, I looked at my hands to see if I was the same person. There was such a glory over everything; the sun came like gold through the trees, and over the fields, and I felt like I was in Heaven.'

Harriet wasn't satisfied with her own freedom, though. She was determined that other slaves should be set free as well. So Harriet volunteered to become one of those brave 'conductors' on The Underground Railroad.

Starting with members of her own family, she went back and forth across the border, leading slave after slave to freedom. This became even more dangerous when the Fugitive Slave Law was passed. The law said that any slaves who had escaped to a free state had to be returned to their masters in the south. But Harriet did not give up, and by the end of her time in The Underground Railroad, she had helped more than 300 slaves find their way to freedom.

She was so good at it, in fact, that William Lloyd Garrison, a famous white man who campaigned for the end of slavery, started calling her 'Moses'. Harriet was thrilled, of course, that she herself was now known by the name of the Bible hero she had admired as a child.

When the American Civil War began – a war that was fought, in part, to end slavery – Harriet volunteered for that as well.

It was the Union Army, the army of the northern states, which was against slavery. So Harriet worked for them, as a nurse and a cook, at first. But with her experience leading slaves out of the southern, slave-owning states, she was so much more valuable than that. She started spying for the Union Army, and discovering where the enemy was hiding. And she even guided a group of the army to a place called Combahee Ferry, where more than 700 slaves were set free!

When the Union Army won the war, and slaves in every part of America were freed, Harriet went to live in Auburn, New York. There, she cared for her elderly parents, worked hard in her church, and joined the movement to give voting rights to women.

Harriet lived until 1913. The former slave, plagued with constant headaches from her head injury but inspired by the Bible stories of freedom, had become a true American hero. And that is why, in 2016, the decision was made to put her face on the American twenty-dollar note, replacing the face of Andrew Jackson. A former president, yes. But also, sadly, a slave owner. It was just one final victory for a modern-day Moses who dedicated her life to helping set people free.

Michael Faraday

You wake up in the morning and you switch on the light.

You put on clean clothes, which were washed in the washing machine, and perhaps dried in the drier the day before.

You wander downstairs and open the fridge. You take out some orange juice, maybe, or a yogurt.

You put a couple of slices of bread into the toaster. Or maybe someone makes you some instant porridge in the microwave.

Everything you just did is only possible because of the discoveries of a scientist who lived two hundred years ago, a scientist called Michael Faraday (1791–1867). If we could look inside his diary at just a few bits, it might read a little like this...

It is 1805. I'm 14 now, and I have just left school. I want to become an apprentice. There is a bookbinder just up the road. He said I could learn how to put books together, and glue the covers on, and repair books that are broken. I wonder if he will let me read them...

...The year is 1812 and my apprenticeship is at an end. I read so many books. And the books about science, in particular, were amazing! My father's a poor man, and he may not have been able to give me much in the way of an education, but he did take me to church. There I learnt how God is the creator of everything, and now I hope to study this wonderful world He made. And I've been given a gift – someone has given me a free ticket to see the famous scientist, Humphry Davy, speak at the Royal Institution...

...I have been to four lectures by Humphry Davy. I wrote as many notes as I could and then put them together into what adds up to a 300-page book. Today I sent it to Humphry Davy himself! I wonder what he will think of it. I would jump at the chance to be his assistant. All the things I could learn, and discover for myself...

...It's now 1813 and good news! Humphry Davy loved the notes I sent him! I have been officially appointed as his assistant! Praise God! Sometimes life takes unexpected turns...

...We are in France. It's 1814. Our first stop on our trip around Europe. We have met with a few other scientists already, and many more meetings are planned. There is one particular complaint I have, however. Davy's wife has been treating me rather harshly. Because her husband belongs to the upper class, and I the working class, she will not let me ride in the carriage with him. She has insisted that I sleep in the same room as the servants. All I want is to be a scientist, and learn as much as I can. But if these people of power and influence do not respect me, how will I ever be taken seriously? Perhaps I am being a fool, even thinking I could be a scientist...

...The year is 1815 and we are back from our trip, and I am so glad I continued on, despite my doubts. I have just begun a series of experiments. If God made the universe in an orderly way, then there must be laws that make everything work – laws for us to discover...

...It's been a while. It's 1821 and I have discovered electromagnetic rotation. Simply put, you can make a piece of metal rotate or spin if you pass electricity round it in just the right way...

...It's 1823. Another discovery! If you take certain liquids and heat them so that they become gas, the containers that hold them turn cold...

...Now it is 1831 and I have discovered something fascinating. A combination of movement and magnets can create an electric current...

Electromagnetic rotation is what makes every electric motor work – like the motor in a microwave, which makes the glass plate spin! Michael's second discovery is the very thing that makes every refrigerator work! And finally, when other scientists could only make electricity by mixing chemicals in a battery, Michael had his third discovery – which is still how the electricity is made that lets us turn on our lights in the morning and toast our bread!

World-changing as they were, those were only three of the things that Michael Faraday discovered. And as the number of discoveries grew, so did his reputation. He wrote about his work, and he talked about it, too. In fact, Michael created a series of talks in which he explained scientific ideas to young people in ways that they could easily understand.

Like Davy before him, Michael became a member of both the Royal Institution and the Royal Society, in spite of the fact that he did not belong to the upper class. (You have to wonder what Davy's wife thought of that!) And he was also invited to join academies of science in America, Sweden, France and the Netherlands.

The fact is that the bookbinder apprentice became the most important scientist of his time. His curiosity, love of books, and determination drove him to never give up on an experiment until he found what he was looking for. But there was one more thing that made Michael a great scientist – his love of God and the world He'd created.

So the next time you switch on a light or open the fridge, remember Michael, the man who changed the world as he knew it.

Florence Nightingale

When you go to the doctor's surgery or a hospital, you usually see a nurse, don't you? There are nurses everywhere, doing all kinds of important things to make their patients well. You may know that nurses need lots of special training. They work very hard. And they make a huge difference to the people they help.

When Florence Nightingale was your age, however, there weren't any nurses. Not really. Ex-servants or widows, who couldn't find any other work, tried to help people who were ill. But they weren't properly trained. Plus, most people didn't want to go to hospital anyway. Doctors didn't know much about germs, so nobody washed their hands, or cleaned the tools used for operations. People only went to hospital if they really had to, and many died there, simply because of the conditions.

Back then, in the early 1800s in the UK, girls didn't get much of an education – even those from rich families, like Florence. They were expected to marry men and raise children. The idea of jobs or careers was very strange.

Yes, things were quite different. But thanks to Florence, a lot of that changed...

The first change had a lot to do with her father, William. He was a wealthy landowner who thought that girls ought to be educated, as well as boys. So he taught young Florence Italian, Latin, Greek, history and, most unusually for that time, writing and maths. So it was no surprise that she wanted to put that education to good use when she grew up.

There was another reason as well. Florence was a Christian, and when she was 17, she had what Christians describe as a 'call from God'. She believed that God was asking her to devote her life to serving other people. She was convinced that she could do that best by becoming a nurse – a proper nurse. Her mum and her sisters thought that she should get married, like all the other girls her age. But her father gave her enough money to live on, so she could do what she wanted.

Florence more or less taught herself nursing. She studied science, and read all she could about the best ways to care for sick people. And because she was able to travel, she went to a religious community in Germany that was caring for sick people, and learned a lot there as well.

The first test of Florence's learning came during the Crimean War – a war that took place near the Black Sea between 1853 and 1856. In the first year, Florence was sent by the British government, with a group of nurses she had trained, to a place called Scutari in Turkey, where wounded British soldiers were being treated.

What she found shocked her.

For every one soldier who died from the wounds he received in battle, there were ten more who died because the conditions in the hospital were so awful. The place was filthy. The sewers didn't work. There was hardly any fresh air. And the wounded soldiers weren't properly fed. So serious diseases like dysentery and typhus and cholera spread through the hospital with deadly results.

Florence, her nurses and others set to work. They cleaned up the hospital, fixed the sewers, and made sure the soldiers ate more nourishing meals. And the number of deaths went down in a big way.

Word got back to England of this nurse who went, lamp in hand, all through the night, from one wounded soldier's bed to another, doing everything she could to help them.

Newspapers got hold of the story, and they started to call Florence 'the lady with the lamp'. Soon everyone was talking about her.

She wasn't interested in that though, and she was the first to admit that the changes in the hospital weren't all down to her. But she did see this as a chance to help people understand what real nursing was all about. So something called the Nightingale Fund was established to raise money for the training of nurses. And by the time Florence got back from the war, there was £45,000 in that fund, which would be something like three or four *million* pounds today!

With all that money, Florence was able to start the Nightingale Training School at St. Thomas' Hospital in London. Soon, nurses were using the same methods that Florence had developed in that war hospital. And hospitals were transformed from dirty places no one wanted to go to, into places where people could actually be made well.

But that wasn't all Florence did. She wrote books, lots of them. Perhaps the most famous being *Notes On Nursing*, which clearly explained what good nursing was all about, in ways that everyone could understand. It was the book that students read in her training school, but it was also used by people and families in their homes.

And Florence didn't stop there! She campaigned for cleaner conditions for people all across the world, because she knew that cleanliness, fresh air and good food were the keys to good health – and everybody deserved that, no matter how much or little money they had.

So the next time you go to the doctor's surgery and see a nurse, you might like to ask them if they took an oath when they became a nurse. They might tell you that they took the Nightingale Pledge: a promise to care for their patients to the best of their ability, to do them no harm, and to be the very best nurse they can be. A promise named after Florence who believed, even when she was 17, that God was calling her to a life devoted to helping other people. A promise that she kept, her whole, long life. And a promise that changed the world.

William Wilberforce

You know what a triangle is, don't you? It's a shape with three sides. Why don't you draw one with your finger, in the air or on the floor?

Way back in the 1700s, there was a very important kind of triangle.

The first line of the triangle stretched from the coast of England down to the coast of Africa. Ships would carry all kinds of things that had been made in Britain: copper, cloth, guns and bullets. When the ships got to Africa, those things would be traded for people. African men and women, and even children, would be captured, bound with chains, and then herded into the same ships that had carried all those manufactured goods.

The second line of the triangle stretched from the coast of Africa, right across the Atlantic Ocean, to the islands of the Caribbean. There, the African men, women and children who had survived the sea journey would be sold as slaves to people who grew crops, both on those Caribbean islands and in America. The slaves would work for nothing, often beaten and hurt, growing sugar and cotton and tobacco.

And finally, the third line of the triangle stretched from the Caribbean islands back to Great Britain. The ships that had carried the slaves were loaded with all that sugar and cotton and tobacco, which they carried back to England, and sold.

That route was called the Triangle Trade. It went on for two hundred years, and made lots and lots of money, both for people who lived in Britain, and for the country itself. There was only one problem with it. It was a problem you can probably see, clear as the nose on your face. It was all about selling people – as if they were no more valuable or important than copper or cotton or linen or tobacco. You can see how wrong a system it was. But the people who made money from it couldn't see that at all. Or maybe they just didn't want to. So someone needed to help them see it. And one of those 'someones' was a man called William Wilberforce. If he were to write a letter to us today, it might go something like this...

Dear reader, I'm writing to tell you something rather important. There was a time when I cared little about other people. I was born in Hull, in 1759. My father sadly died when I was nine but my aunt and uncle took me in. They were committed Christians who taught me about Jesus. However, when I went to university, I forgot all of that. My uncle and grandad died, and the inheritance I received from them made me very rich. So, instead of sticking to my studies, I spent my time gambling and drinking and generally messing about. It was a bit like that story Jesus told – the one about the young man who received a lot of money from his father, and then wandered away from doing what he knew was right. (It's called 'The Prodigal Son' if you would like to read it.)

God had a plan for me, though, and thankfully I met some people who set me on the right path. I became good friends with William Pitt (little did we know he would later become Prime Minister). We were both very interested in politics and I became a member of parliament.

I later went on a tour of Europe with my friend, Isaac Milner. As we travelled, we read and discussed a book that was all about Christianity. All that I had learned about Jesus from my aunt and uncle came back to me. And much like that young man in the story Jesus told, I realised that my life was nothing like the life God wanted for me. So I said sorry for the things I had done and I determined to live for God. Part of that meant changing my personal habits like gambling and drinking. And part of that meant changing what was wrong with the world around me.

And that's where meeting Thomas Clarkson made all the difference. He was also a Christian, and could see that the whole idea of slavery was evil. He and others had formed a group to try to bring an end to slavery. They knew that, if that was ever to happen, they would need the support of people in the government, like me. So, Thomas showed me exactly what slavery was like.

He explained how the slaves were crowded into the holds of the ships that carried them – chained together and packed so tightly they could hardly move.

He explained how those conditions resulted in the spread of horrible diseases among the slaves.

He told me how thousands upon thousands

of those poor African people died on the way to America. And that's before they were subjected to the beatings that many of the people who worked as slaves on the American plantations received.

And perhaps most important of all, he made it clear how wrong the slave traders were.

It may be hard to believe, but those slave traders and owners actually convinced themselves that slaves weren't properly human. But Thomas showed me that those slaves were people, just like me – who deserved dignity and respect. So I decided to do something to help change things.

When we got started, it seemed like it would be too hard to make slavery itself something that was against the law. But we thought that if we could first make the buying and selling of slaves illegal, then that, in turn, would end slavery. If we could stop the Triangle Trade, stop people making money, then they would stop trading slaves.

So I did two things. I took wealthy and powerful people on tours of slave ships to show them the awful conditions the slaves had to suffer. I wanted them to see it for themselves, just as I had.

And second, because I was in government, I began to introduce laws that would make it illegal to buy and sell slaves. I stuck to it, not for one or two years, but for 20 long years. And finally, in 1807, Parliament passed a law that made it illegal for British ships to carry slaves.

That was just the beginning, though. Having won that victory, my friends and I decided it was time to make slavery itself against the law. So, once again, I went to work. And 26 years later, when I was 73, I received word that Parliament had decided to abolish slavery throughout the British Empire.

People finally saw what I and others had seen. Slavery is simply wrong.

May you too, dear reader, discover what is wrong – and do what you can to make it right.

Yours, William

Three days after slavery was abolished in Great Britain, William Wilberforce died. He worked tirelessly for the rights of others. Today, sadly, people are still being bought and sold as slaves (we call this 'trafficking') in many parts of the world. In fact, there are more slaves today than there were in William's day. So, perhaps it's time for us to be Wilberforces, too.

Elizabeth Fry

On the back of an English five-pound note,
there is a picture of Winston Churchill. He was
Prime Minister of Great Britain during the Second
World War. Most people know who he is.
But if you looked at the back of one of the
old five-pound notes, you'd see a picture of
a woman called Elizabeth Fry. Who was she?
Why did she deserve to be honoured and
remembered in the same way as Churchill?

Elizabeth was born Elizabeth Gurney in 1780, into a family of wealthy bankers. Her father was one of the men who ran Gurney's Bank, which you probably haven't heard of, because it doesn't exist anymore. But her mum was from the Barclay family, who ran Barclay's bank, which you can still see on the high street. Perhaps an adult you know uses their bank today, or you have watched them use one of Barclay's cash machines?

Elizabeth's family belonged to a group of Christians called Quakers. When Elizabeth was 18, she heard a sermon – a talk – by an American Quaker called William Savery. He was an abolitionist, which means that he wanted to bring about an end to slavery. And, like many Christians, he really wanted to help the poor.

Young Elizabeth was moved by Savery's talk and decided that she would help the poor, as well. She visited people living in poverty in Norwich, where she lived. She collected clothing for them. And she started a Sunday school, which was a different thing in her time than it is today.

Today, children go to Sunday school to learn about God and Jesus and the Bible. In Elizabeth's time, only wealthy children could afford to go to school. Children from poorer families went to work as soon as they could instead. So Sunday schools were set up by Christians to teach those children to read and write. And that's what Elizabeth did.

In 1800, Elizabeth married Joseph Fry, a tea trader, and moved with him to London. Elizabeth and Joseph would have 11 children in all, so she had quite a lot to do during the early years of her marriage. Still, she managed to qualify as a Quaker minister, and she gave talks encouraging her audiences to help the poor.

In 1813, Elizabeth visited the women's area of Newgate Prison. She was horrified by what she found there. The prison was overcrowded, dirty, violent and filled with disease. Prisoners slept on straw mats and had to cook their own meals. And, worst of all, there were children in the prison. That's right. If your mum was sent to prison and there was no one else to care for you, then you had to go to prison too!

Elizabeth was determined to change all that. She took food and clothing to the prisoners. Then she set up a school, so the children could get an education. She taught the women how to sew and knit, so they would have a way to make money when they left the prison. She believed that prison shouldn't just be about punishing people, but about helping them find a different and better way to live.

She even stayed in the prison overnight, and invited other wealthy people to stay with her, so they could see for themselves how awful the conditions were.

Finally, she started an organisation called the British Ladies' Society for Promoting the Reformation of Female Prisoners. Yes, it was a mouthful! But it gave other women the opportunity to improve the prisons. And it was, in fact, the very first British national women's organisation, ever.

It wasn't long before the newspapers started writing about this wealthy woman who spent time in London's grimiest prison. They called her 'the angel of the prisons'. As a result, some very famous people were drawn to her cause. Queen Charlotte, the wife of King George III, invited Elizabeth to her house. And when their granddaughter, Victoria, became queen many years later, she too encouraged and supported Elizabeth's work.

Elizabeth also became the first woman to make an official speech to Parliament. The government was trying to pass laws that would make prisons better. Elizabeth argued for something that is common practice today – that women, not men, should be in charge of guarding women prisoners. In 1823, the Gaols Act was passed by Parliament, and Elizabeth's suggestion about women guards became law. The Act also introduced prison visits by Christian ministers, an end to the use of heavy leg irons, and wages for prison guards, who had been paid by the prisoners themselves before that. That's right – if you went to prison in those days, you had to pay your own guards!

Elizabeth's work became so well known that she was invited to visit prisons all across Europe to make suggestions for improving them as well.

If that is all that Elizabeth had done with her life, it would have been amazing. But Elizabeth had been genuinely changed by that Christian sermon she'd heard as a young woman. And as she looked, she could see that there were so many more things that needed changing in the world around her.

In the winter of 1819, for example, she saw the body of a dead homeless boy, lying in the streets. So she set up what she called a 'nightly shelter' in London, where homeless people could sleep, safe and warm.

She went to Brighton and started something called the Brighton District Visiting Society, which sent volunteers regularly into the homes of poor people to see what they needed.

And she established one of the very first schools for training nurses. In fact, it was from Elizabeth's school that Florence Nightingale recruited her first group of nurses.

So that's why Elizabeth Fry's picture was on the back of the old five-pound note. Her faith in God inspired her to make a huge difference in the time and place she lived. And there's no reason why you can't make a difference, too. Take a look around you, like Elizabeth did. Spot the things you see that are wrong, that are hurting people. Ask yourself, 'What can I do to change that?' And then do something!

Thomas Barnardo

You have probably seen people wrapped up in blankets, huddling in doorways, maybe asking for money. Homeless people are sadly still a common sight in most British cities and towns.

Imagine, for a moment, what that must be like. You have no place to live. No TV to watch. No table, no sofa, no chairs. And unless you can find a place to sleep in a homeless shelter, you have to sleep outside – no matter how cold or wet it is.

You have probably never seen someone your age homeless – but there was a time in the UK when thousands of children were. For many children, life was not at all easy.

Thomas Barnardo, who was born in Ireland in 1845, decided to do something to help those without homes or families. He set up homes for children to come and live, learn and grow. Let's find out more about this man...

When Thomas was 16, he became a Christian. A year later, he went to hear a talk given by a famous Christian missionary called Hudson Taylor. Missionaries travelled all over the world, helping people and telling them about Jesus. Thomas was so impressed by the things Hudson Taylor was doing that he decided he wanted to be a missionary to China, just like his new hero. So he went to London to train as a doctor.

You will sometimes hear people referring to Thomas Barnardo as 'Doctor' Barnardo. The truth is, though, that Thomas never finished his training, and never officially became a doctor. And that is because something happened to change his 'mission' in life.

While he was training, a dangerous disease called cholera broke out across London. Three thousand people died from it. As a result, many children lost their parents and had to sleep in the streets. That wasn't the only reason, of course. There was already a lot of poverty and homelessness in London at the time. The spread of cholera just made things worse.

It all caught Thomas' attention. He could see the poor children as he made his way to the hospital each day, and he felt sorry for them. So he decided to do something about it.

The first thing he did was to set up what he called the 'Ragged School'. It was held in a donkey shed, of all places! Up to 200 children would come, two nights a week, and on Sundays. Thomas would teach them to read and to write, and because it had made such a difference in his life, he would also teach them from the Bible.

One winter's evening, a boy in the class hung around after the lessons were finished, sitting close to the warm stove. When Thomas asked him what he was doing, the boy led him outside and down an alley, to the roof of a nearby building where 11 other boys were sleeping rough. At that moment, Thomas wondered if God really did want him to go all the way to China. It seemed like there were plenty of needs for him to meet in London, on his own doorstep.

Thomas shared his concerns with Lord Shaftesbury, who was a Christian like Thomas, and a politician. Lord Shaftesbury encouraged Thomas to do everything he could for the poor children of London. And when another politician gave Thomas a lot of money to help him find a property where the homeless boys could live, Thomas knew that his life's work would no longer be in China, but in London's East End.

At first, Thomas rented a place big enough for 25 boys. He didn't want to take in more children than he had the ability to care for properly. One night, when the house was full, he turned a boy away. And only a few days later, he discovered that the boy had died in the night, cold and hungry. So Thomas decided that, from then on, he would never turn away anyone who needed his help. And that is why, step by step, he started buying houses all over London, so there would be room for even more boys!

In 1873, Thomas married Sara Louise Elmslie, whose nickname was Syrie and who was also a committed Christian, devoted to caring for the poor.

Thomas' work with boys was going well, but there were also many girls who had to sleep rough in the streets, and were in danger. So, together, Thomas and Syrie set about providing safe housing for girls as well.

Syrie came from a wealthy family, and as a wedding present, the couple were given a big house that sat on 60 acres of land. It was perfect! So they turned the house into a home for girls and they set about building cottages over the rest of the land to take in more girls. They not only provided homes for those girls, they taught them skills so they could earn their own money.

Thomas and Syrie had children of their own as well. One of their daughters was born with Down's syndrome. Thomas and Syrie learned a lot about her special needs, and their homes became famous for taking in and caring for children with disabilities as well.

No one will ever know what would have happened had Thomas Barnardo gone to China. But there is no question that he made a difference in London. By the time he died, in 1905, Thomas and his wife had set up 96 homes and taken in over 8,500 children.

And his work lives on today. A charity, simply called Barnardo's, still meets the needs of children all over the UK. It does amazing things – things that never would have happened had Thomas Barnardo not listened to God and changed his mind.

Corrie ten Boom

Perhaps you have a big wardrobe at home, or a big cupboard at school. Now pretend (don't actually do it!) that you and five of your friends had to go into that wardrobe or cupboard and stand there, perfectly still, for an hour. You can't sit down. You can't move. And you can't make a sound.

It would be uncomfortable, wouldn't it? (And smelly, maybe, if one of your mates had bad breath or passed wind!)

Now imagine that you were only in there because soldiers were searching for you, going from room to room, guns at the ready, in case they found you and you tried to escape.

That would make the whole thing even more uncomfortable, wouldn't it? And frightening. But while you might find standing in that tiny space uncomfortable and difficult and scary, you would probably also be grateful for it. Because it was the only thing keeping you safe and alive.

There once was such a hiding place. It was above a watchmaker's shop, in the city of Haarlem in the Netherlands, built at the back of a room where the watchmaker's daughter slept. Her name was Corrie ten Boom. Let's hear her story...

In 1892, a girl was born – the youngest of four children. Her family went to church and her parents put their faith into action by providing food, clothes and shelter for the poor. When Corrie grew up, she followed in their footsteps and started a youth club for teenage girls, where they were taught the Bible and learned how to sew.

Corrie learned how to make watches as well, just like her father. And she became the first ever official female watchmaker in Holland (a region of the Netherlands).

In 1940, when Corrie was 48 years old, something terrible happened. The Second World War had begun the year before, and now the German army were invading her country. Holland soon fell under the control of Adolph Hitler, who was the leader of the Nazi political party. One of the things the Nazis did when they conquered a country was to arrest all of the Jewish people. The Nazis hated Jewish people. They blamed them for all that was wrong with the world. And they had plans to put them all to death.

The Nazis were terribly mistaken about this, of course. But imagine, for a moment, how awful it would feel if the government hated you just because of your parents' race or where your parents had come from. And then imagine how you would feel if the government had plans to arrest you, put you in prison and kill you. You'd want somebody to stand up for you, wouldn't you? To hide you and protect you and save you.

That is exactly what Corrie's family decided to do for the Jews. They knew their Bibles, remember? So they knew that Jewish people were precious to God. And they set about doing what they could to save them.

The watchmaker's shop was the perfect place for this rescue operation. Customers would come and go all the time. It was always busy. So word went round that Jewish people could walk into that shop and find a safe place to stay. Sometimes they stayed for an hour or two. Sometimes they stayed for a few days. And then, usually, they were sent to another safe home to stay.

But when the German soldiers were spotted, searching for Jewish people in the neighbourhood, someone in the shop downstairs would press a buzzer, and the people upstairs had one minute to go to that hiding place, built into a wall at the end of Corrie's bedroom.

If the soldiers came into the shop, the people hiding would have to be absolutely still and absolutely quiet. There was a little vent built into the hiding place, so they could breathe fresh air, but still it was very hard and very frightening.

For four years, Corrie's family hid Jewish people and those who were fighting to get the Nazis out of Holland. In that time, Corrie became a leader in organising safe houses all around the Netherlands. And the best guess is that her family saved over 800 people in that watchmaker's shop alone.

But then, early in 1944, someone told the Nazis that Corrie's family was hiding Jewish people. The soldiers burst into the shop, not to find Jews this time, but to arrest the whole ten Boom family. What the soldiers didn't know was that someone had pushed the buzzer. So the people in the hiding place were not found, even as Corrie's family was being dragged away. They stayed there, in that tiny hiding place, for three whole days! And then they were rescued by those fighting against the Nazis.

Things did not go so well for Corrie and her family, though. Her 84-year-old father was sent to one prison camp, where he died almost immediately. Corrie and her older sister Betsie were sent to another prison camp, where they held Bible studies and tried to encourage the other prisoners.

The conditions in those camps were dreadful, and in December of 1944, Betsie died as well. Her faith in God stayed strong, though. And she believed that God was with her, even in that terrible camp.

Twelve days later, many of the other women in the prison camp with Corrie were killed. But she was set free, possibly because a clerk had made a mistake.

So when the war ended and the Nazis were defeated, Corrie set about telling everyone what had happened in those prison camps. She wrote a book about her experiences, called *The Hiding Place*. And she set up groups to help not only the people who had suffered in those camps, but also the people who had actually helped the Germans!

That might seem strange to you, but Corrie believed in what Jesus taught, and so she believed we should forgive each other.

Forgiving doesn't mean saying, 'What you did was OK, don't worry about it' – it's more like saying, 'You made a mistake, but I make mistakes too. I'm not going to stay angry with you, I'm going to treat you as God would want me to.'

Corrie's book became very popular and she was invited to speak all around the world. In Germany, one evening, she was standing at the back of a church, shaking hands with people who had come to hear her. A man reached out his hand and thanked her for her words. And the minute she saw him, she recognised him. He had been one of the Nazi guards at the prison camp where her sister died.

'Jesus has forgiven all the wrong that I have done,' he said to her. But all Corrie could think about were the awful things he and his fellow soldiers had done to the prisoners. Corrie prayed a prayer, and then realised that Jesus had indeed died to forgive everyone, even this man – and that she should forgive him too. So she reached out her hand and took his. And in her own words, this is what happened: 'As I took his hand the most incredible thing happened. From my shoulder along my arm and through my hand, a current seemed to pass from me to him, while into my heart sprang a love for this stranger that almost overwhelmed me... When (God) tells us to love our enemies, He gives, along with the command, the love itself.'

Corrie ten Boom died on her birthday in 1983, the day she turned 91. Jewish people believe that dying on your birthday is a sign that God has blessed you. One thing is certain: Corrie was a blessing to the hundreds and hundreds of people she and her family saved, and to the millions who have been inspired by her story of bravery and forgiveness.

When Martin Luther King Jr was a boy, growing up in Atlanta, Georgia in America, his father took him to a shop to buy him some shoes. When Martin had chosen the shoes he wanted, his father went to pay for them.

'Sorry,' said the person on the till. 'You'll have to pay at the back of the shop. This till is for white people only.'

Martin's father was furious. He did not go to the back of that store to pay. No. He put down those shoes and walked out.

It was unfair. And Martin never forgot that, nor the way that his father stood up to the unfairness.

It wasn't the first time, and it wouldn't be the last. For everywhere that Martin looked, he was surrounded by unfairness.

In Atlanta in the 1930s, African-Americans had to drink from different water fountains than white people. And use separate toilets. And go to different schools. And sit at the back of the bus. Segregated. That's what they called it. Different treatment for different people, just because of the colour of their skin.

If Martin could tell his story to us today, it might go a little like this...

My father was a preacher in a Baptist church. His real name was actually Michael King. And when I was born, I was called that too. But when I was five, my father went to Germany, and was so impressed with the work of the German Christian, Martin Luther, that he took his name and gave it to me as well!

I loved music, and was a member of the church choir. I was a good student too. Public speaking was one of my favourite subjects. I did so well I was actually allowed to skip two years of school. And I went off to university when I was only 15! While I was there, I decided to follow in my father's footsteps. I knew that Jesus stood up for the poor and the outcasts, and people who were not treated fairly. So I figured that being a preacher would be the best way to fight the unfairness around me.

With that in mind, I moved to Pennsylvania to study. And then to Boston. While I was in Boston, I was introduced to a talented music student called Coretta Scott, who would soon become my wife!

When I graduated, I was asked to become the pastor of the Dexter Avenue Baptist Church in Montgomery, Alabama. And it wasn't long before

I was using my position to fight those unfair segregation laws.

That battle to make things fair for African-Americans was called the Civil Rights Movement. Some people wanted to make that battle an actual battle. They wanted to use violence to change the system. But I knew that Jesus wouldn't have used violence. So I organised peaceful protests and marches to bring about change.

One day in 1955, an African-American woman called Rosa Parks, who also lived in Montgomery, was riding the bus. The seats for African-Americans were at the back of the bus, and the seats for white people were at the front. But the law said that if the seats for the white people filled up, then African-Americans had to give up their seats if more white people got on. That's what happened to Rosa. She was sitting where she was supposed to, but the white section was full. So when the next white person boarded the bus, the driver told her to give up her seat. But she refused. She knew she was breaking the law, and she was arrested for doing so. But she was fed up with the unfairness. I heard all about this and decided to lead a boycott of the buses.

And so, for 385 days, African-Americans refused to ride the buses in Montgomery.

The people who wanted to keep segregation were furious. Someone bombed my house, and I was sent to jail. But, in the end, the US courts decided that the bus company was wrong. They put an end to the segregation bus laws, and people could sit where they wanted, whatever the colour of their skin.

News of this victory spread all across America. People started to listen to me, so I spoke about the Civil Rights Movement and the need to change the laws. Along with others, I formed the Southern Christian Leadership Conference in 1957, which encouraged churches to oppose segregation in a non-violent way. Slowly but surely, that approach won support among people of all races.

You might have heard about or seen pictures of the biggest non-violent protest I organised. In 1963, over 250,000 people gathered and marched in Washington, and that is the place where I gave a speech that many call 'I Have a Dream'. In it I said, 'I have a dream that my four little children will one day live in a nation where they will not be judged by the colour of their skin but by the content of their character.'

Because of those marches and that speech, the US Congress passed the Civil Rights Act of 1964, which did away with segregation in all public places. So people could use the same toilets, drink from the same water fountains, go to the same schools and work in the same places, whatever their race.

Martin never gave up fighting for fairness. And in 1964, he became the youngest person ever to receive the Nobel Peace Prize.

Very sadly, in 1968, while supporting a protest against low wages and poor working conditions, Martin was killed. He was standing on a balcony when a man, who had escaped prison, shot him. He was only 39 years old.

But people did not forget him – the boy in the shoe shop who grew into a man with a dream. And that is why every year, on the third Monday of January, there is a national holiday where Americans remember his birthday, and are reminded of all that Martin Luther King Jr did to turn a dream into action and make a fairer world.

Catherine Booth

A boy noticed a group of homeless people sleeping on the banks of the River Thames. When he told his dad about them, his father's response was simply, 'Go and do something.'

It's one thing to notice a need – it's another to act and do something about it, isn't it?

The father's name was William Booth and he founded The Salvation Army. You might have heard of them or seen them around. At Christmastime, you may see them playing in a brass band and wearing their uniforms.

So who are they? 'Salvation' sounds like a churchy word. And 'army'... well, that sounds like a fighting word, doesn't it? So why are they together? The answers can be found in the lives of a husband and a wife, William and Catherine Booth.

Let's see what we can find out about Catherine in particular...

Born in Derbyshire in 1829, Catherine grew up in Lincolnshire and in London. She was never very healthy. She had a problem with her spine and her heart and her lungs, which meant she had to stay in bed quite a lot. She went to school for a bit, but when that proved too difficult with her illness, Catherine was taught by her mum.

Her parents were committed Methodist Christians – which in part meant they worked hard to care for the poor. Sadly, however, Catherine's father ran into hard times and turned his back on his faith. He drank a lot of alcohol and became addicted to it. That made life even more difficult, both for him and for his family.

Despite all this, Catherine dedicated her time to helping people. Even as a young teenager, she wrote articles for magazines, encouraging people not to drink alcohol.

Catherine loved to read. In fact, by the time she was 12, Catherine had read the whole Bible eight times! (Do you know anyone who has read the Bible that many times? Why not ask your local vicar or pastor if they have?!)

But Catherine didn't actually become a Christian until she was 16. She read a line of a

Christian song and it just jumped out at her – and she realised that she belonged to God.

In 1852, William Booth came to speak at Catherine's church. And three years later they were married! William was very good at talking about God – even when he was a teenager. Like Catherine, William believed in doing all he could to make a better world. He encouraged the people to feed and clothe the poor, to fight for justice and equal rights. But there was one particular area where William needed Catherine's help to achieve more equality between men and women.

In those days, it was very rare for a woman to preach a sermon – to give a talk – in church. Catherine did not think that was fair. And it wasn't! She had read the Bible eight times through, remember? So why couldn't she teach others about it?

When she told William that she wanted to stand up in church and give a talk, he was not keen on the idea. In fact, he was very much against it. Catherine did not give up, though. In the middle of a church meeting, Catherine believed that God was telling her to speak.

So up she stood, and out the sermon came. William was amazed. It was an incredible talk! So from that moment, Catherine spoke regularly, and people rushed to listen to her wherever she went.

In 1865, Catherine and William started The Christian Mission in the East End of London, which eventually became The Salvation Army. They preached sermons in the streets, out in the open. They cared for the poor and homeless – those whom other, more respectable people seemed to despise.

Crowds began to flock to this kind of Christianity. It served the poor and spoke to ordinary people in ways they could understand. In Salvation Army meetings there was singing and clapping, all set to the music of, you guessed it, brass bands!

As many would have understood what it was like to be part of the British Army, The Salvation Army was organised in a similar way. William was known as the General, and Catherine as the Army Mother. Both men and women preached and worked together as leaders.

The Salvation Army became so popular that by 1882, there were more people going to their meetings in London than any other kind of church. That gave Catherine the chance to make even more changes in the world around her. She discovered women and children working in terrible conditions, for up to 11 hours a day, hidden away in the London slums. They received hardly any money for the work they did. It was called 'sweated labour'; today, they would be called 'sweatshops'. So Catherine set about improving those conditions and challenging the people they worked for to pay them a fair wage.

Catherine also found that women who made matches were suffering from a terrible disease. It was all down to the stuff they used to make the matches burn. But there was a safer way of making matches that caused no disease at all. So Catherine worked hard to change that, and in the end, The Salvation Army started its own match-making factory, so the workers would be safe.

In spite of her ill health, and all the work she did, Catherine gave birth to eight children, seven of whom – boys *and* girls – became famous Salvation Army preachers. Catherine wrote at least six books and countless magazine articles, and was involved in the very early stages of the campaign to give women the right to vote.

In 1890, Catherine died after two years of battling cancer. For an amazing person, an amazing number of 38,000 people came to her funeral!

The Salvation Army is still going strong today! Still very much inspired by faith in God, it is working in 128 countries to serve communities, help those in need, and fight for justice.

Every year they help more than 2,500 people to find employment, reunite 2,000 families, provide 3,200 homeless people with a bed each night, and serve 3 million meals to those who need them most – and that's just in the UK!

Catherine, William, their family and The Salvation Army didn't just notice the need around them, they did something about it. It's simple, really, but what a change it makes!

Cecil Jackson-Cole

Have you ever gone into a charity shop? Some high streets have lots of them.

Maybe you looked through the children's books. Or picked up the toys. Or tried to find a DVD. Or maybe you helped your mum or dad unload boxes and bags full of things from the boot of the car – things they wanted to give to the charity shop. And maybe some of the things in those boxes were your old books or toys or DVDs!

That's how charity shops work. People give them things they no longer need. Then the charity shops sell those things, and the money they get goes to help people with all sorts of needs. Elderly people. People who are ill. Animals that are sick or need homes.

Some help people all around the world, who simply don't have enough to eat. That's what a charity called Oxfam does. Let's hear from the man who started the very first Oxfam shop. In fact, it was the very first charity shop of them all!

I was born Albert Cecil Cole, but you can just call me Cecil!

Things were very different in 1901 – when I was born in the East End of London. There were hardly any cars at all. There were no televisions. Only rich people had telephones in their homes. And nobody had even thought of computer games or mobile phones.

Lots and lots of people were very poor, and that was certainly the case with my family. My father tried to make money. He started many different businesses but they weren't very successful. And that meant my family had to keep moving from place to place, every time one of the businesses failed. That was really hard for me. I never stayed in one school for more than nine months. Think of that: having to get used to different teachers and make new friends, over and over and over again...

In 1914, my father went off to fight in the First World War. Somebody had to earn money for the family – the government didn't have a system to help people who had very little money back then – so, at the age of 13, I left school and went to work. Maybe you have an older brother or sister who is 13. Can you imagine them going off to work every day, and making enough money to provide for your family?

I found a job at a business that sold vegetables to shops. It wasn't much to start with. But, unlike my dad, I turned out to be quite good at business. Very good, actually, if I do say so myself! So, by the time I was 18, I was in charge of a whole team of salesmen.

Things didn't stop there, either. My father had returned from the war and was running a furniture shop. But, like his other businesses, it was sadly failing. So I bought that shop, and made a success of it. In nine years' time, there were four more of those shops dotted about London.

A very sad thing happened during those years. My mother died. I loved her very much. And I missed her. So I decided to take her maiden name, Jackson, as my middle name, and from that time on, I was always known as Cecil Jackson-Cole. Or CJC.

I was not only dedicated to running my businesses. I was dedicated to following Jesus – I was a Christian, you see. I knew that Jesus cared about helping people in need. So I decided that would be the point of my business as well. I would earn money to help others.

And so, in 1932, I bought a big house and turned it into a place where soldiers who had served in the war could stay if they needed a rest.

Just before the Second World War, I moved to Oxford and opened one of my shops there. Some very important men in that city got together to help people in Greece, who were starving because of the war. They asked me to help. And this seemed like another good charity for me to get involved with. It was called 'The Oxford Committee for Greek Famine Relief'.

When the war was over, many of the men who ran that charity thought its work was done. But I knew there were many more people around the world who were starving. So I convinced those involved that they needed to keep going. And so 'The Oxford Committee for Greek Famine Relief' became Oxfam, dedicated to helping hungry people everywhere!

The problem, as I saw it, was how to raise enough money to keep the charity going. The answer I found was to do something that no one had ever tried before – to try what was successful in business in the charity.

Salesmen went from door to door, trying to sell things. So why, I thought, shouldn't charities do the same, asking for donations instead? And businesses ran shops. So why shouldn't charities open shops as well? That is when the idea for the very first charity shop was born. The shop was in Oxford (of course!) and, in no time at all, it was earning more money for the charity than anyone ever believed was possible. And so more shops popped up, all around the country.

I wasn't satisfied with that, though. After the war, many ordinary people could afford to buy houses. This was a new thing. And it was a good thing. But the business of buying and selling houses was quite old-fashioned, and mostly aimed at rich people. So I started Andrews, one of the very first businesses designed to help ordinary people buy houses. And all the money we made went towards other charities I founded.

Charities like... Andrews Charitable Trust, which helps community projects... Help the Aged, which helps the aged (of course!)... Anchor Housing, which provides homes for elderly people... Action Aid, which was the very first charity to encourage people to sponsor individual children around the world. And there's the Christian Book Promotion Trust, which is very important to me. Learning about Jesus has made all the difference in my life, and I want other people to have that chance as well. So, the Christian Book Promotion Trust made Christian books available to schools and libraries.

Today, the Christian Book Promotion Trust is known as Speaking Volumes. And this very book is one of their projects! Have you enjoyed reading it?

You might ask, did Cecil get a big award for all he did – a knighthood or some other honour? Not at all. He didn't really want that sort of thing. He lived a very quiet life. But by the time he died in 1979, he had made an enormous difference to millions upon millions of people he had never met. And that is probably the most important honour of all.

So the next time you go into a charity shop, ask your mum or dad if they have ever heard of Cecil Jackson-Cole. It's likely they won't have. But then you can tell them his story. The story of a man who started those charity shops. And who really did make a world of difference.

Our sincere thanks to...

Author Bob Hartman, who was game for the project from its inception and who researched and re-told the lives of the people in this book in his legendary way.

Rebecca Parkinson, Educational Advisor and Site Editor of Assemblies Online, who gave input on content to meet the curriculum, age-appropriate language and style and wrote all the additional teaching material and assembly plans that accompany the book.

The team at CWR, headed by Lynette Brooks, Director of Publishing and Ministry, including Katie Carter, Lead Editor and Simon Ray, Creative Services Team Leader. And Anna-Marie Glover for her expressive illustrations.

Alexandra McDonald, Commercial Director of SPCK and CBPT trustee who gave much advice and direction when needed.

Years 2 and 3 of St Aidan's Catholic Primary School, Coulsdon who gave us lots of useful feedback during our visit.

Friends in the teaching and publishing business who helped shape the book: Eileen Henderson, member of Speaking Volumes' book selection panel, Suzanne Blackburn-Maze, Deputy Headteacher at Duxford School, Cambridge, and Andrew Hodder-Williams, Publishing Director of Lion.

And finally, to the trustees of the Christian Book Promotion Trust and Andrews Charitable Trust for providing funding and support to make this book possible.

The trustees would like to thank Paula Renouf for all her diligence and hard work in making this project happen.

**speaking
volumes**
Placing good books in your community

This book was written on behalf of the
Christian Book Promotion Trust in celebration of
their 50 years of providing books on the Christian
faith to libraries and schools through the
Speaking Volumes scheme.

If you would like to know more, or benefit from
funding for more Christian books please visit
www.speakingvolumes.org.uk

Additional copies of this may be purchased from
www.cwr.org.uk/shop

Additional teaching resources for this book are
available at **www.stapleford-centre.org**

Additional assembly ideas are available at
www.assemblies.org.uk

CWR Applying God's Word
to everyday life and relationships

CWR was founded as a Christian ministry in
1965 by Selwyn Hughes. Since then, we have
grown into an international publishing and
training organisation based at Waverley Abbey
House in Farnham, Surrey. Our main activities
include providing books and resources based
on the Christian faith for all ages, courses
to encourage and equip Christians to live
their daily lives God's way, and training for
counsellors through our educational arm –
Waverley Abbey College.

If you would like to find our more, visit
www.cwr.org.uk

All our books and resources for children can be
found at **www.cwr.org.uk/children**